Are You Contemplating Selling Your Toronto Rental Property?

Get The Best Capital Gains Tax Advice For Smart Investors

Thomas Cook

ABOUT THE AUTHOR

Let's start off by giving you a little background about where I'm coming from in terms of experience and knowledge. I've been in the real estate industry since 1980. While originally with Royal LePage, I switched to RE/MAX Hallmark in 1983, where I have been ever since.

Along with helping literally thousands of people to buy and sell their homes, over the years I've been involved in a number of other real estate related activities as well. For example, through the '80s I had a property management company and at times managed up to 350 single-family homes, duplexes, triplexes, condos, and small four- and eight-unit buildings, mainly for investors but often for people who were out of the city on a job transfer and wanted to maintain their existing residence.

That has provided some great insight into such things as tenant related issues, understanding of the Tenant Protection Act, and knowledge on how to design a really good rental application and a comprehensive lease. I find those things help today with clients who are interested in buying something that has a rental component to it — maybe the traditional basement rental apartment where the owner lives upstairs, or more likely today a downtown Toronto condominium suite.

I've renovated about twenty-five homes in Toronto, as well as building a triplex from the ground up in Riverdale. In 2008, I built a cottage in the Kawarthas that started with an uncleared lot. These experiences certainly provided some great insights into working with contractors, dealing with City Hall for building permits, and even on occasion going to the Committee of Adjustment or the OMB (Ontario Municipal Board) when obtaining a permit requires applying for a variance.

I find these experiences help with clients who might be interested in buying something that needs renovation or fix up work.

I can certainly offer advice and answer those kinds of questions for my clients — and many more.

For several years, I also had a mortgage company, which provided a lot of insight into mortgage financing and learning how to package the buyer's mortgage application to get clients the best possible rate and terms.

During my 37+ year career, my Team and I have helped over 2500 buyers and sellers reach their real estate goals. This achievement has earned me one of the highest RE/MAX sales production awards... the Circle Of Legends.

TORONTO'S REAL ESTATE TEAM
MISSION STATEMENT

Our goal is to give you such an exceptional home selling or buying experience that you will feel compelled to tell all your friends and family about us.

We use our time each and every day to its fullest potential, always remembering that our clients pay us to work diligently to get their home sold, or find their next home for purchase.

We strive to deliver more value to you than you expect to receive and to provide uncompromising service based on integrity, fairness, knowledge, professionalism and enthusiasm.

Once your real estate transaction has been completed, we'd be honoured if you were to refer our services to everyone you know so they could share the same excellent experience you enjoyed.

HERE'S HOW TO GET IN TOUCH...

Thomas Cook
Real Estate Sales Representative @ RE/MAX Hallmark Realty Ltd
Brokerage

Mobile | 647-962-1650
Office | 416-465-7850

LivingInToronto.com
Direct | Thomas@LivingInToronto.com

Author | Ultimate Toronto Home Buyer's Guide
Author | Toronto Home Buyer's Financing Guide
Author | Free Government Money Report
Author | Insider Tips For Getting The Best Price
Author | Best Capital Gains Tax Advice
Author | Guide To Attracting The Best Tenants
Author | Guide To Downtown Toronto Condo Prices

Experience || Thousands of homes sold since 1980
Professional Designations || ABR, SRES
Awards || RE/MAX's 2ND highest award - Circle Of Legends
Charity Support || Over $117,500 contributed to the Toronto Sick Kids
Hospital
Speaker & Agent Coach || Delivering seminars and presentations to the
public and Realtors about buying and selling real estate since 1995.

CONTENTS

FOREWORD…

As a Realtor who frequently assists people who own investment real estate, I often get asked questions about the capital gains tax on the sale of their property.

To create this report, many thanks go to Chris Makris from Robert Gore and Associates, Chartered Accountants in Toronto who I interviewed to get the information I'm going to provide to you now.

An investment condominium or house is defined as a property which has been rented out for a length of time and, at some point in time during the ownership period, it was not the owner's prime residence.

Anyone who owns an investment condo or house will need to face paying capital gains tax to the federal government on the profit they realize when they sell their property. This applies to both Canadian residents and non-residents.

Of course, you should be getting your final capital gains tax advice from your own professional accountant or attorney but this report will serve as an excellent reference when talking to them.

There are several common scenarios so let's review them.

Thomas Cook
Real Estate Sales Representative @ RE/MAX Hallmark Realty Ltd
Thomas@LivingInToronto.com

SCENARIO ONE – A CANADIAN PURCHASES A PROPERTY STRICTLY FOR INVESTMENT

The first scenario would be the simplest, where a condo or house investor buys a unit, never lives in it as their prime residence, and rents it out for their entire ownership period before they decide to sell their investment.

That's the most common situation. For the owner, the most important documents to collect and keep right from the beginning, is what it cost you to buy that property.

A lot of people assume that you just need the closing documents from the initial purchase. However, it's also possible to deduct other expenses relating to the acquisition including any travel expenses and the buying research time. It's just like starting a business.

A lot of people don't just start their business and begin invoicing the next day. They've researched it for several months beforehand. All the costs leading up to that purchase can be added to the cost base of that investment condo so that, down the road, they will help to reduce any possible capital gains tax expense.

These expenses could include a mileage calculation on your travel, parking costs etc. In some cases, accountants have seen people claim part of their internet expense… doing research on the MLS for example.

Of course, any hard expenses directly incurred on the purchase such as a home inspection, legal fees, land transfer taxes, etc can all be added to the purchase cost basis.

These ancillary expenses don't give us major tax savings, but they add up. For example, let's imagine that you're in the highest tax bracket, you've been looking for three or six months and you've spent a lot of time researching and driving around to meet up with your agent.

Let's say those expenses total $2,000 or even $3,000. On that $3,000 expense, that could work out to a savings of up to 53% (top tax bracket) on $1,500 or about an $800 tax saving.

It doesn't sound like a lot, but every dollar saved counts. Nobody wants to give their gain back to the government. You want to try and keep as much of it as you can.

Some people choose to deduct those 'soft' costs against ongoing rental income but the Gore accountants don't recommend it. The Canada Revenue Agency (CRA) prefers that you calculate those expenses and then add them to the original purchase cost of the condo.

Let's take an example where you paid $300,000 for a condo including all acquisition expenses and then you held onto it for six years and then sold it for $500,000. That $200,000, the difference between what you sold it for and what you paid for it, is your capital gain.

Your taxable capital gain, the amount that you pay taxes on, is 50% of your actual gain.

In the example here, that amount then would be $200,000 x 50% = $100,000. The amount of actual tax that you pay on that $100,000 is determined based on your other sources of personal income.

If your regular taxable income is below $50,000, you will pay tax at a rate of 20% on the taxable amount of the capital gain, or 10% of the whole gain. If you're in the highest tax bracket, which is anything above $200,000 in annual taxable income, you will then pay 53% on the taxable capital gain, or 26.5% on the entire gain.

So, it's really that simple.

Everyone's goal is to reduce the amount of that capital gain by applying legitimate deductions throughout the ownership period. You can also add in any capital improvements you've done to the condo or house IF you haven't already deducted them against any rental income.

On the sale, you can again deduct your legal fees plus all Realtor expenses and any other closing costs.

It's very important to keep all your ownership documentation for the entire ownership period. After selling, you should have two sets of closing documents from your lawyer plus receipts for every deductible expense incurred along the way.

A question often comes up as to whether you should take depreciation of the property while you own it.

The office policy at Gore's practice is to deter you from taking depreciation which can only be deducted from any cash flow surplus annually.

Why? Let's say you take a $5,000 depreciation every single year for five years. In the year of sale, the $5,000 annual deduction that you've taken is now going to be 're-captured' and added back onto your sale price.

By taking that depreciation along the way you've gone from having a deduction of $5,000 per year against positive cash flow, to now having an income inclusion of $25,000 in the year of sale, along with the possible capital gain.

Remember depreciation on a property can only be claimed up to the point of bringing your rental income positive cash flow down to zero. You can't create a loss with it.

Gore's office has had situations where clients have had just a small depreciation number, say $1,000, and the clients have said, you know what, I'll deal with that recapture when I sell.

But in most cases, clients were considering much larger annual depreciation numbers of five, ten or fifteen thousand dollars... substantial amounts... and that always comes back to bite you when you ultimately sell that investment property.

By having to add that 'recapture' onto your capital gain, you could've moved yourself from, say the second lowest bracket or the lowest tax bracket, to now possibly the highest bracket.

Gore and Associates always discourage it, unless there's a financial reason why someone doesn't want to report any taxable income in a tax year.

If you're a Canadian resident owning and selling a property, you could also use capital losses from prior years to offset any capital gains you're liable for now.

So, if you've had stock market or real estate losses in the past, where you've sold an investment and lost money, those capital losses get carried forward for the rest of your life, and can be deducted from this new real estate capital gain to reduce your final taxable capital gain.

They've seen situations where clients have done very well on real estate, but where the clients have suffered is with a couple of bad investments on the stock market.

Usually, they will sell those bad investments prior to the year-end and recognize a loss to help offset the gain against the property sale.

SCENARIO TWO - NON-RESIDENT INVESTORS WHO SELL THEIR CANADIAN PROPERTY

The next scenario to consider would be the situation where the investor never lived in the condo or house. In fact, they're not Canadian residents. What differences come into play in this scenario when related to capital gains?

A non-resident must file a Section 216 Canadian tax return annually to declare the income from their investment property.

On that form, you need to show your rental income, your rental expenses, and you file a tax return just like everybody else does. You get no special deductions attributable to a Canadian resident tax payer, but you still get to deduct all the expenses relating to the property as you always would.

When it comes time for you to sell, you must complete what's called the CRA T2054 form, which documents every expense from the beginning of when you bought it and the rental income that you earned.

Then there's a tax calculation that's done at the very bottom of that form which helps determine what your capital gains tax will be. Even though the investor is not Canadian, they still must file a Canadian tax return to detail the final disposition of that property.

From a tax point of view, a non-resident investor will pay a little more capital gains tax because of the fact they don't get the same basic exemptions which every Canadian tax payer gets, but overall, it's not that bad.

Normally the completion and filing of the CRA's T2062 document is handled by the seller's lawyer. Their lawyer will take in all the information with respect to the purchase and selling expenses. The investor's accountant still must file their Section 216 form, where they just show the final ownership year's rental income and expenses.

From a capital gains taxing standpoint, a non-resident is treated exactly the same way as a Canadian resident. Calculate the difference between what you bought it for (plus expenses) and what you sold it for net and then 50% of it is taxable… the same as it would be for a Canadian.

Then you would pay the final capital gains tax at a tax rate depending on the size of your taxable capital gain.

By the way, in all the scenarios we're presenting here, every investor needs to keep copies of all their acquisition, ongoing and disposition expense receipts.

You should keep all those receipts for seven years from the date the final CRA Notice of Assessment is received. That technically makes it eight years. Rule of thumb, normally it's necessary to keep those records for three years because the CRA will only go back two to three years unless they suspect fraud.

And if there's fraud, or malicious intent to avoid paying the proper tax (what's called GAR or general anti-avoidance regulation), they then can knock down that wall of three years and go back as far as they want. But the rule of thumb is two to three years.

There's Federal Government Reporting Required Now On Every Canadian Real Estate Sale

One question that often gets asked is how does the government protect themselves to make sure they collect on that capital gain when a property is sold by a non-resident?

In the past, it was the one area where the government was very sloppy. As a result, in 2016 the CRA started forcing everybody to document all their real estate sales on their annual tax return, including their prime residence.

Because what was happening was, you would have investors/renovators buying several properties frequently and registering the title in the names of various family members… the wife, husband, son, daughter, nephew, etc.

Then everybody claimed their principal residence deduction on the sale of those homes, even though in some cases they never lived in them.

They could get away with selling those investments and designating them as their personal homes and thereby recognizing no profits and paying no capital gains taxes.

CRA now basically says, if you sell any home, and even if it's designated as your principal residence, there must be full disclosure.

And the disclosure information requirement is the year you purchased it, the full address of the property, and how much you sold it for.

And if you don't disclose a real estate sale, there's an $8,000 penalty, and you run the risk of CRA taking away that entire principal residence exemption, and making it fully taxable.

Gore's office has had a few clients who were quite reluctant to disclose the sale of their home. They were fearful they were going to be taxed. They were cautioned that if they didn't disclose, they risk being taxed even more.

Capital Gains Tax Money Gets Collected At Closing

How does that capital gains tax get collected if the property is sold this year but the seller doesn't have to file a tax return until the following calendar year?

There's an automatic 25% withholding tax that's collected by your lawyer representing you on the sale. So, if a non-resident sells a property, one of the requirements by the seller's lawyer handling the actual transaction is to withhold 25% of the entire transaction selling price.

If the sale price is $1,000,000, the lawyer is going to hold on to $250,000 of the proceeds until the T2054 form is filed and the taxes are calculated.

For simplicity, if that $1M property was purchased for $400,000, there's a $600,000 capital gain of which $300,000 is taxable (50% remember) which results in a maximum tax liability of just over $150,000 (50% of 50% = 25%).

Since the seller's lawyer is holding back 25% of the 'gross' sale price, the CRA is protected against people not paying their proper tax.

The 25% holdback works in CRA's favor of course. They always require that the seller's lawyer withhold more than what's needed to pay the actual tax and thereby force you to do the paperwork before you can get the balance of your money back. It's very smart.

You don't have to wait until the following year to file your final tax return to get the money back. The seller's lawyer just needs to complete and file the T2062 form right away after the sale.

SCENARIO THREE – A CANADIAN RESIDENT LIVES IN THE PROPERTY FOR A PERIOD OF YEARS AND THEN TURNS IT INTO AN INVESTMENT PROPERTY

How does that capital gains tax get collected if the property is sold this year but the seller doesn't have to file a tax return until the following calendar year?

There's an automatic 25% withholding tax that's collected by your lawyer representing you on the sale. So, if a non-resident sells a property, one of the requirements by the seller's lawyer handling the actual transaction is to withhold 25% of the entire transaction selling price.

If the sale price is $1,000,000, the lawyer is going to hold on to $250,000 of the proceeds until the T2054 form is filed and the taxes are calculated.

For simplicity, if that $1M property was purchased for $400,000, there's a $600,000 capital gain of which $300,000 is taxable (50% remember) which results in a maximum tax liability of just over $150,000 (50% of 50% = 25%).

Since the seller's lawyer is holding back 25% of the 'gross' sale price, the CRA is protected against people not paying their proper tax.

The 25% holdback works in CRA's favor of course. They always require that the seller's lawyer withhold more than what's needed to pay the actual tax and thereby force you to do the paperwork before you can get the balance of your money back. It's very smart.

You don't have to wait until the following year to file your final tax return to get the money back. The seller's lawyer just needs to complete and file the T2062 form right away after the sale.

Get A 'Move-Out' Valuation Done By A Realtor You Trust

Or you could calculate your capital gains tax applicable number this way.

You can ignore your original purchase price and get a market valuation done on the property as of the date that you moved out and it became a rental. You deem the property to have been 'sold' as of that date under your principal residence deduction. That 'move-out' value then becomes the new cost base for your investment.

From our example above, you will only pay capital gains on the difference between what you sold it for in 2015 versus what it was appraised for in 2008 when you got the 'move-out' valuation done.

The investment property owner of course still needs to back up their claim by keeping records of all their income and expenses.

Remember that during the period of renting the property, you can deduct any repair expenses against rental income. It's better to do it this way because you're getting a full dollar for dollar deduction.

Gore's accounting team would rather see a taxpayer be aggressive in a sense of being able to deduct the expenses every year against rental income, rather than saving them up and only getting 50% of the value of a deduction applying them against a capital gain on the sale.

Capital gains are the best tax you can pay because, really, you're only being taxed on half the income, and the other half is free. No other income we earn in Canada is treated this way.

You should take full advantage of very opportunity, and remember, you have to recognize this income as capital gains.

Gore's office has had clients who refused to sell shares because they were worried about paying the capital gains tax. They've also had clients who didn't sell a property for exactly that same reason.

It's amazing how people react when they have an opportunity to put a million dollars in their pocket, but it could cost them $120,000 in capital gains tax. Some folks can't bear the thought of writing a cheque to the CRA for $120,000 although they're still putting a big cheque for $880,000 in their pocket. It sometimes keeps them from making that selling decision.

Can You Defer Paying Capital Gains?

There are a few other nuances as to when capital gains tax is due and payable.

For example, a request from the buyer for the seller to take back a mortgage for part of the purchase price may not happen so often these days with our low interest rates but it's possible.

Let's say the buyer is having trouble coming up with conventional financing but you're very happy with the selling price AND you don't necessarily need the cash coming out of the sale.

As the seller, you could take back a mortgage (VTB or vendor-take-back) for a portion of the purchase price. You can defer paying capital gains on that VTB for five years.

Here's how that works.

Let's say you take back a VTB mortgage of $300,000. You can differ the recognition of a capital gain, divisible by 1/5 of the vendor take-back mortgage, for five years.

Therefore, in this example you could defer paying tax on the whole $300,000 and just pay tax on $60,000 (1/5th of the $300K) of your capital gain every year.

This is better than recognizing all $300,000 as taxable in the year of sale.

YOUR NEXT STEPS GOING FORWARD…

1. Collect all your purchase documents and ongoing expense & income receipts and have them ready to present to your lawyer and/or accountant
2. If you lived in the rental property for a period of time, call us to get a '**Move-Out Valuation**' done as of the date you started renting the suite. You can have us do this for you anytime and you don't have to wait until you decide to sell. It's better to have this in your hands and kept with your other ownership documentation.
3. When you start to think about disposing of your rental property, call us to do a **Room-By-Room Review** where we'll do a walk-through of your suite or house to make cosmetic-only suggestions as to what should be done to maximize your selling price.
4. Hire us to sell your property with our '**Breakthrough Marketing With A Guaranteed Difference**' marketing plan
5. **Send referrals**… you'll want your friends to have the same great real estate experience you're having ☺

Thomas Cook & Partners
Toronto's Real Estate Team
Real estate sales representatives @ RE/MAX Hallmark Realty Brokerage

Office | 416-465-7850
Mobile & Text | 647-962-1650
Email | Thomas@LivingInToronto.com
Web | www.LivingInToronto.com

Robert Gore and Associates – Robert & Mary Gore and Chris Makris
Call the office at 416-699-8070 or email Chris@Goreca.com

AMAZING FREE SERVICES AVAILABLE
TO TORONTO BUYERS & SELLERS

People always have questions when they're starting to search for real estate or when they want to sell what they have.

Toronto's Real Estate Team has designed many resources to help buyers and sellers through their real estate experience.

There are complementary books and reports to download and many free services available depending on where you are in the buying or selling process.

Take a look at which of our 'Free Stuff' opportunities is perfect for you right now...**FreeStuff.LivingInToronto.com**

HERE'S THE FREE STUFF YOU CAN GET FROM US

Exclusively For Toronto Condo Or House BUYERS...

Helping Toronto Home Buyers Achieve Their Goals Since 1980

Sometimes people start thinking about buying real estate years ahead and others jump right in and purchase a new condo or house in just a few months. Either way, it makes sense to spend some time learning the right way to buy and avoiding making costly mistakes on one of the biggest purchases of their life.

Our Home Buyer University has created several ways for you to improve your knowledge about the home buying process and how Toronto's real estate market works right now.

Enroll in as many of these options as you'd like and be all set to go when the time is right for you.

Perfect If You're 6-24 Months Away From Buying A Toronto Home

It always pays to get prepared. We've designed a Buyer University educational series with articles either bi-weekly or monthly designed to teach condo and house buyers about the home buying process in Toronto in a systematic way.

Go to **HomeBuyerUniversity.ca** and complete the Buyer University registration.

Timeline = 6-24 months before purchasing

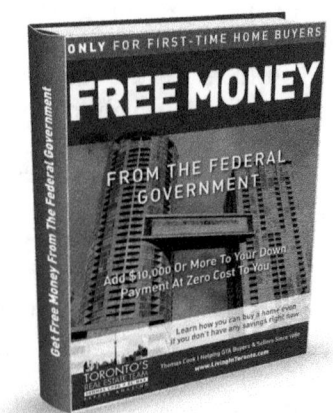

Create A Down Payment Even If You Have Nothing Saved Right Now

Would you like to buy your first Toronto

condo or house but don't have a large, or any, down payment saved right now?

Our Free Government Money Report will show you how to grow or add to your down payment if you're a first-time home buyer.

Download it for free at **FreeGovernmentMoneyReport.com**

Timeline = 6-24 months before purchasing

Home Buying Advice For 1st-Time Or Experienced Buyers

Do you like to understand how something works before committing to it?

The Ultimate Toronto Home Buyer's Guide will take you through the entire home buying process in a comprehensive way and help take away the stress of buying one of the most expensive purchases in your lifetime.

Download the Guide for free at **UltimateHomeBuyersGuide.com**

Timeline = 3-18 months before purchasing

Get MLS Listings Sent To You Daily Just Like Realtors See

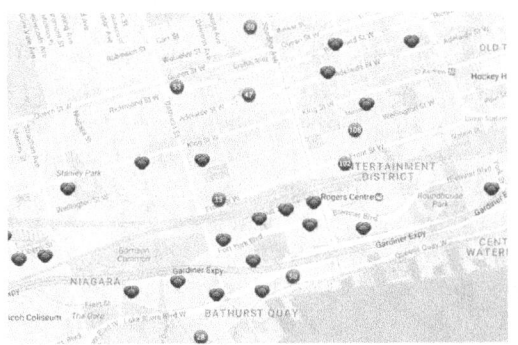

The customized HOMEWatch Program is perfect if you are several months away from seriously starting your home search.

Instead of randomly looking for homes on your own, you'll get information by email on all the new listings that come on the market in any price range and Toronto neighbourhood you choose.

Go to **CustomHomewatchSearch.com**

Timeline = 3-12 months before purchasing

Are You Wondering What You Should Do First?

Buying a home can be a confusing enterprise and many people don't know the best place to start. A Starbucks Strategy Session is a casual over-a-coffee conversation where you'll get your big and small questions answered to give you some terrific clarity about what to do next.

Remember, to achieve any goal you need a plan. The Starbucks Strategy Session is the best first step in setting up that plan.

Sign up at **StarbucksStrategySession.com**

Timeline = 4-16 months before purchasing

Look At Properties Without Needing Your Cheque Book

When most folks are just starting to think about buying a condo or house, they typically don't have an accurate idea of what they can get for the

money. They're often worried that they're too far away from the time they want to seriously start looking and don't want to bother an agent to see some homes just for the experience.

The Market Experience Tour is designed to help you get a feel for what's out there in the market in the neighbourhoods and price ranges that you feel comfortable with, without you having to worry about bringing your cheque book along.

This Tour is not designed to find your dream home… it provides an opportunity for you to get educated and find out what home styles, layouts and price ranges work best for you well before you're ready to seriously start your home search.

Market Experience Tours happen almost every day of the week… just pick the time, price range and neighbourhoods that suit your lifestyle.

Visit **MarketExperienceTour.com**

Timeline = 4-16 months before purchasing

How Large A Mortgage Do You Qualify For?

Often people mistakenly think that going to an online site or having a quick, casual conversation with a bank rep to find out everything they need about getting a mortgage approval but this is absolutely not the case.

The perfect solution to getting a full mortgage pre-approval is to have a private, in-depth conversation with a mortgage professional who will review your personal financial situation and offer options about the best way to move forward.

A typical Mortgage Consultation takes about 20-30 minutes and you'll walk away with a mortgage pre-approval that you can feel confident about. Sign up at **FullMortgagePreApproval.com**

Timeline = 3-9 months before purchasing

Here's A Simple Way To Save Time And Money When Starting Your Home Search

OK, so now you're ready to start seriously looking for your new home.

You've read up about how the home buying process works, you've been receiving some targeted listings from various Toronto neighbourhoods, you've been on a few (or several) Market Experience Tours to get a feel for the current market and your full mortgage pre-approval is in place.

The next big step is to meet up with your buyer agent for a comprehensive, in-office or online Buyer Consultation so you're fully prepared when you hit the bricks looking for that perfect condo or house.

A **Buyer Consultation** with an experienced, professional agent should take approximately 60 minutes… there's a lot to cover and understand and you don't want to make any mistakes or get stressed out in the process.

Go to **BuyerConsultation.com**

Timeline = 3-5 months before purchasing

Exclusively For Toronto Condo Or House SELLERS…

Sometimes people start thinking about selling their property years ahead of time and others jump right in and sell their condo or house within a few days or weeks.

Either way, it makes sense to spend some time learning the right way to sell and avoiding making costly mistakes on one of the biggest sales of their life.

Now that you've read this book, you certainly have a clearer idea of how the entire home selling process works but there are still a few important things you need to do. Our **Home Seller University** has designed some terrific ways for you to profitably proceed with the sales process.

If you are going to sell your home in the next 1 to 9 months, what you undertake right now can make a difference of thousands of dollars in your sale price, and there are some simple things you can do forthwith to make sure you get "Top-Dollar" when you do sell.

A Quick Way To Find Out What Your Condo or House Could Be Worth In Today's Market

Before you start making any plans to move up, move down or move out to a rental, you'll need to know a market value price for what your home is worth in today's market.

The best way to do this is to have us complete a FREE **Pin-Point Price Analysis**, where I can take a closer in-person look at your condo and prepare a very specific price for your suite.

This price will be more precise than the general range that you can get automatically from any website - and we guarantee in writing to sell your condo at the Pin-Point Price or higher in less than 32 days.

Go online to **PinPointPriceAnalysis.com** and fill in your property's specifics... it's that easy

Timeline = 1-12 months before selling

Increase Your Home's Value With Simple Cosmetic Fix-Ups

So, you're happy with the price you could get... what's next?

The absolute best next step is for us to do a FREE "Room-By-Room Review", where I take a 20-minute walk-thru of your condominium and make specific recommendations about which fix-ups or improvements you should (and should not) do to prepare your suite for sale.

I will point out the lowest cost, highest return improvements you can make to help sell your condo quickly and for more money.

Set up your Room-By-Room Review at **RoomByRoomReview.com**

Timeline = 1-4 months before selling

Sell Your Condo In As Little As 24 Hours - And Laugh To Yourself At How Easy It Was

Some home owners are sensitive to having a lot of people traipsing through their home or there's some limitation as to their putting the condo on the public MLS system.

If that's you, one solution is to include your condo in our "Silent Market" of condominiums that are not yet on the open market.

Because we generate so much buyer interest from our website, Facebook and Google advertising and other proactive marketing, we may be able to find a buyer for your condo without even putting it on the market... saving you both time and money.

Register your condo 'silently' for sale at **SilentMarketForCondos.com**.

Timeline = 1-3 months before deciding to put your condo on the MLS system

---

Insider Tips For Getting The Best Price - The Complete Guide To Selling Your Toronto Condo

By reading this book you're on your way to helping yourself have a successful sale and

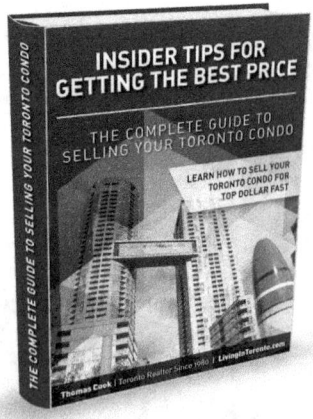

getting the highest price possible. As the saying goes 'Knowledge Is Power'. In this book, I will be telling you how my Team and I approach selling Toronto homes.

I've worked through three recessions since 1980 and now one of the longest stretches of market appreciation in Toronto's history.

So, I've seen it all... extreme buyer's markets and now extreme seller's markets... but in every instance, a competent, knowledgeable Realtor adds value to every seller when they're ready to enter the market.

Download the Book for free at **GettingTheBestPrice.ca**.

Timeline = 3-6 months before selling

Are You A Toronto Condo Investor?

Finding the right tenant for your rental suite is critical to having a profitable investment.

Mistakes made in the tenant selection process can end up costing you thousands of dollars in lost rent, legal fees or damage repairs.

Ontario's tenancy laws tend to protect the tenant's rights far more than the landlord - even if the tenant is clearly at fault.

It's essential to know exactly what must be done right when renting out your condo suite.

Download the Book for free at **GuideToAttractingTheBestTenants.com**.

Timeline = ANYTIME you own an investment property

APPENDIX - CRA DOCUMENT

Canada Revenue   Agence du revenu
Agency   du Canada

Request by a Non-Resident of Canada for a Certificate of Compliance Related to the Disposition of Canadian Resource or Timber Resource Property, Canadian Real Property (Other than Capital Property), or Depreciable Taxable Canadian Property

INSTRUCTIONS – T2062A

All legislative references are to the Canadian *Income Tax Act.*

When and How to file the Form

Use this form if you are a non-resident of Canada to give notice of the proposed disposition of, or the completed disposition of, Canadian resource property, Canadian real property (other than capital property), Canadian timber resource property, or depreciable Canadian taxable property. A disposition of taxable Canadian property includes any interest or option for such property, whether or not the property exists.

Use Form T2062 for the proposed or completed disposition of other taxable Canadian property, including the gain on the disposition of depreciable property. If both forms T2062A and T2062 are required for a disposition, the forms must be filed together.

If you are reporting a proposed or completed disposition of Canadian resource property, you must also complete Form T2062A, Schedule 1, *Disposition of Canadian Resource Property by Non-Residents.*

File a separate T2062A for each disposition or proposed disposition. However, if you are disposing of, or proposing to dispose of, several properties to the same purchaser at the same time, only one T2062A is required for all the properties. A separate T2062A must be filed by each person indicating an interest in a joint tenancy, tenancy in common, or co-ownership.

We issue a certificate of compliance after tax is paid or security acceptable to the Minister is submitted. You may have to file a Canadian income tax return to report the disposition of property listed on this form. Final settlement of the tax liability is made when you file your Canadian income tax return. Failure to attach the certificate of compliance to your income tax return may result in a delay in processing. For further information related to the filing requirements, please refer to the CRA website.

Completing the Form

Send this notice along with all supporting documents (see list attached), to the Centre of Expertise (CoE) for the area where the property is located. If there is more than one property and the properties are located in several areas and more than one CoE is affected, the notification should be sent to the CoE where the majority of the properties are located. If the property is real property, the CoE is determined based on the property's legal or municipal address. If the property is shares or assets in a business, the CoE is determined based on the head office address of the corporation whose shares are being disposed of, or where the business is located. If the property is a capital interest in an estate or a trust (pursuant to the distribution of capital), the CoE is determined by the location of the trustee. The CoEs are listed on the CRA's website: **cra.gc.ca/nrdispositions#whrfrm.**

Vendor Information

Country of residence – Indicate the country where you normally, customarily, or routinely live.

Identification number – Enter the appropriate identification number. This will ensure that security or payment made for tax is credited to the correct account. Identification numbers must be used when filing your Canadian income tax return and on all correspondence with us.

Social insurance number (SIN)	– applies if an individual was formerly a resident or a deemed resident of Canada.
Individual Tax Number (ITN)	– is a number assigned to a non-resident individual who filed a Canadian income tax return in previous years.
Subsidiary ledger number	– is a number assigned to a non-resident individual who has made a remittance but does not have a Canadian tax account number.
Business number (BN)	– is a registration number for businesses such as corporations, partnerships, and sole proprietorships.
Trust account number	– is a number assigned to a trust that filed a Canadian income tax return in previous years.

If you do not have a SIN or ITN, please complete Form T1261, *Application for a Canada Revenue Agency Individual Tax Number (ITN) for Non-Residents,* available on the Internet at **cra.gc.ca.** Include the completed form and supporting documentation with your T2062.

Applying for a BN

Complete Form RC1, *Request for a Business Number (BN).* Form RC1 and our pamphlet, *The Business Number and Your Canada Revenue Agency Accounts,* are available on the Internet at: **cra.gc.ca.**

Send the completed RC1 with a copy of the certification of incorporation to the Centre of Expertise where you filed the Form T2062.

Details of property – If a disposition includes more than one property, attach a piece of paper providing the details for each property. All amounts must be in Canadian dollars.

    Property jurisdiction – include the city/municipality, province/territory, and postal code for the street address requested below in "Property description".

    Property description – include the following details:

        Depreciable property, real property (other than capital property) and timber resource property – street address, plan number, lot number, registration number, serial number, and use of property (rental, lease, or business); a written description and the applicable class of asset according to Schedule II of the *Income Tax Regulations.*

        Resource property – well or mine location, legal description, and street address.

Gross Proceeds of Disposition

Enter the gross proceeds of disposition from the sale of the property. Enter the vendor's share of the gross proceeds in Column (1).

Proceeds of disposition (Column 1) and Capital Cost (Column 2)

For dispositions of depreciable property, enter amounts in columns (1) and (2) and enter the lesser of columns (1) and (2) in column (3).
For dispositions of timber resource property and real property (other than capital property), enter the proceeds of disposition in column (1) and in column (3).

T2062A E (11/2016)   (Vous pouvez obtenir ce formulaire en français à arc.gc.ca/formulaires.)

Canada

22

Undepreciated capital cost or cost amount (Column 4)

For dispositions of depreciable property and timber resource property, use the undepreciated capital cost. For dispositions of real property (other than capital property), use the cost amount.

Exemption (Column 6)

If you are claiming an exemption from tax, such as under a tax treaty or a principal residence exemption, enter the exempt portion in column (6). If the amount claimed is pursuant to a tax treaty, the vendor has to certify that they are resident in the stated country of residence and, if the tax treaty contains a limitation on benefits provision (e.g., Article XXIX A of the Canada – US treaty) the vendor has to provide written certification that they meet the requirements of the provision in relation to the property described in this form. Please attach a note detailing any calculations involved in determining the exemption amount.

Note: You cannot claim outlays and expenses related to the disposition of property, including real estate commissions, brokerage fees, and legal and notary fees, when you file this form. However, you can claim these amounts when you file your Canadian income tax return.

Certification

This area should be completed and signed by:

- the vendor in the case of an individual;
- an authorized officer in the case of a corporation;
- the trustee, executor or administrator if the person is filing the statement for a trust; or
- an authorized partner in the case of a partnership.

More information

You can get information about residency status in Canada from Interpretation Bulletin S5-F1-C1: *Determining an Individual's residence status*, or by contacting our general enquiries line as follows: From inside Canada or the United States **1-800-959-8281** (for non-resident individuals and trusts) or **1-800-959-5525** (for non-resident corporations), From outside Canada or the United States **613-940-8495** (for non-resident individuals and trusts) or **613-940-8497** (for non-resident corporations). You can also visit our website at **cra.gc.ca**.

You can also get information from:

Information Circular:	IC72-17 – *Procedures Concerning the Disposition of Taxable Canadian Property by Non-Residents of Canada – Section 116*
Interpretation bulletins:	IT-176 – *Taxable Canadian Property – Interests in and Options on Real Property and Shares*
	IT-419 – *Meaning of Arm's Length*
Guide:	T4058 – *Non-Residents and Income Tax*

Supporting Document List

When you send us your completed Form T2062A, you must attach supporting documents so we can process your request. To help you, we have provided the following reference list. You can tick (✓) the boxes that apply to you.

Transactions

Sale of depreciable property

If you sell depreciable property, include copies of:

☐ the sales agreement (actual disposition);

☐ the capital cost allowance (CCA) schedules for all years;

☐ documentation to support the cost amount and capital cost;

☐ a completed Form T2062, *Request by a Non-Resident of Canada for a Certificate of Compliance Related to the Disposition of Taxable Canadian Property*; and

☐ the offer to purchase (proposed disposition).

Rental Property

If you sell rental property, include:

☐ documentation to support the allocation between land and building;

☐ documents to support subsection 21(1) and (3) elections regarding capitalization of interest.

Leases

If you grant an interest in property, or dispose of an interest in property, include copies of:

☐ the right of-way agreement;

☐ the surface lease agreement; or

☐ the leasehold interest agreement.

Vendor takes back mortgage

If the vendor takes back the mortgage, include:

☐ a copy of the mortgage agreement.

Mortgage foreclosures and power of sale

If the transaction is a result of a mortgage foreclosure or power of sale, include copies of:

☐ the power of sale or court order; and

☐ the mortgage agreement.

Sale of Canadian resource property

If you sell Canadian resource property, include copies of:

☐ the petroleum and natural gas lease;

☐ the offer to purchase and conveyance agreement;

☐ Form T2062A, Schedule 1, *Disposition of Canadian resource property by non-residents;*

☐ documents to support pool balances;

☐ the sales agreement (actual disposition); and

☐ the purchase agreement (when property was acquired).

Sale of Canadian timber resource property

If you sell timber resource property, include copies of:

☐ the CCA schedules for all years;

☐ documents to support any revenue received (e.g., logging contract, payments from sawmills);

☐ your Canadian income tax returns for the last three years;

☐ the offer to purchase (proposed disposition);

☐ the sales agreement (actual disposition);

☐ the purchase agreement (when property was acquired); and

☐ the calculation of the ACB.

Sale of partnership property

If you sell partnership property, include copies of:

☐ the sales agreement (actual disposition);

☐ the listing of partners (including their names, addresses, Canadian identification number, percentage ownership and each partner's portion of payment;

☐ the partnership agreement; and

☐ the offer to purchase (proposed disposition).

Partnership interest

If the property is a partnership interest, include:

☐ a calculation of the ACB;

☐ a copy of the partnership capital account balance; and

☐ the purchase agreement (if interest was originally acquired from another partnership).

Partnership residual interest

If the property is a partnership residual interest, include a copy of:

☐ a calculation of the ACB.

Partnership continuing income right

If the property is a continuing income right, include:

☐ the calculation of the ACB; and

☐ documents to support the partner's share of income.

Tax Treaty Exemptions

If you are claiming an exemption under a tax treaty, you have to give us proof of residency.

The vendor has to provide sufficient information to establish that they met the requirement of the treaty and that they are eligible for tax treaty benefits under the treaty. In this regard, the vendor should complete and submit Form NR301, *Declaration of eligibility for benefits under a tax treaty for a nonresident taxpayer*, Form NR302, *Declaration of eligibility for benefits under a tax treaty for a partnership with non-resident partners*, Form NR303, *Declaration of eligibility for benefits under a tax treaty under a hybrid entity*, or equivalent information. For partnerships and hybrid entities, each partner or member in respect of whom treaty benefits are claimed must provide a summary declaration to the CRA as indicated below.

Individuals should include:

☐ copies of their most recent income tax returns from the treaty country; and

☐ a letter from the tax authority in the treaty country confirming their residency status.

Corporations should include:

☐ a copy of their charter;

☐ a letter from the tax authority in the treaty country confirming their residency status; and

☐ copies of their most recent income tax returns from the treaty country.

Hybrid entities should include:

☐ complete and submit NR303, *Declaration of eligibility for benefits under a tax treaty for hybrid entity*, and Worksheet B or equivalent information; or

☐ proof of the election to be taxed as a corporation.

Note: A treaty exemption can only be claimed on the portion of income derived by residents of the United States who are entitled to treaty benefits under paragraph 6 of Article IV of the Canada – United States tax treaty and to whom paragraph 7 of the same article does not apply. These persons must also meet the limitation on benefits provision of Article XXIX A.

Get The Best Capital Gains Tax Advice

Partnerships should include:

- ☐ Complete and submit NR302, *Declaration of eligibility for benefits under a tax treaty for a partnership with non-resident persons*; or
- ☐ proof of the election to be taxed as a corporation.

Trusts and estates should include:

- ☐ a copy of the trust agreement, indenture, or will; and
- ☐ a letter from the tax authority in the treaty country confirming the trust's residency status;
- ☐ copies of the most recent income tax returns from the treaty country.

Fresh start rule

If you are claiming an exemption under the *Canada-US Tax Convention*, Article XIII paragraph 9 (Fresh Start Rule), include:

- ☐ proof that you were a continuous resident of the United States from September 26, 1980, to the date of sale;
- ☐ the value of the property on December 31, 1971 (for property acquired before January 1, 1972);
- ☐ the calculation of the exempt portion of the gain accrued to December 31, 1984; or
- ☐ an appraisal report for the fair market value of the property on December 31, 1984.

Non arm's length transactions

If the transaction is between non arm's length parties, include:

- ☐ an appraisal report determining the fair-market value of the property at the time of disposition; or
- ☐ a letter of opinion from an appraiser or agent.

Gift of property

If the transaction is a gift of property, include:

- ☐ a copy of the transfer deed.

Section 85 elections (rollovers)

If a section 85 election is made on the transaction, include a copy of:

- ☐ a Form T2057, *Election on Disposition of Property by a Taxpayer to a Taxable Canadian Corporation*; or
- ☐ a Form T2058, *Election on Disposition of Property by a Partnership to a Taxable Canadian Corporation*; and
- ☐ all supporting documents including variations, appraisals, and calculations showing how the agreed amounts were determined.

Corporate reorganization

If the transaction is a result of a corporate reorganization, include:

- ☐ copies of documents explaining the reorganization;
- ☐ a list of steps involved in the reorganization; and
- ☐ a corporate organization chart.

Deemed dividends – section 212.1 or subsection 84(3)

If a section 212.1 or subsection 84(3) deemed dividend results from the transaction, include the calculation of the:

- ☐ deemed dividend or paid-up capital reduction;
- ☐ tax paid up capital; and
- ☐ non-resident tax account number.

Trusts and estates

If the vendor is a trust or estate, include the following information as well as documents related to the transaction:

- ☐ name and address of the trustee, executor, administrator, or other representative of the trust or estate;
- ☐ proof of residency of the trustee, executor, administrator, or other representative of the trust or estate;
- ☐ list of beneficiaries and their residences;
- ☐ the trust or estate's country of residence; and
- ☐ disclosure that a trust is a party to the transaction.

Charities and non-profit organizations

If the vendor is a charity or non-profit organization, include the following information as well as specific documents related to the transaction:

- ☐ proof that the organization is registered as a charity for tax purposes in the country of residence.

Joint tenancy, tenancy in common, or co-ownership

If the vendor is a member of a joint tenancy, tenancy in common, or co-ownership, include the following information as well as specific documents related to the transaction:

- ☐ a list of names and addresses of all members; and
- ☐ the percentage of ownership of each member.

Elections

If you previously made an election on the property, include a copy of the election form such as:

- ☐ Form T2061A, *Election by an Emigrant to Report Deemed Dispositions of Taxable Canadian Property and Any Resulting Capital Gain or Loss.*
- ☐ Electing under subsection 45(2), deems the change in use from personal to income producing not to have occurred.
- ☐ Electing under subsection 45(3), deems the change in use from income producing to personal not to have occurred.

Note: If there was a change in use and no election was made, provide the fair market value of the property at the time the change occurred.

Payment of tax or security

If you are making a payment of tax, include:

- ☐ the trust cheque, certified cheque, bank draft, or money order;
- ☐ the bank guarantee; or
- ☐ proof that acceptable security has been provided to the Minister.

Thomas Cook

I◆I Canada Revenue   Agence du revenu
      Agency   du Canada

Request by a Non-Resident of Canada for a Certificate of Compliance Related to the Disposition of Canadian Resource or Timber Resource Property, Canadian Real Property (Other than Capital Property), or Depreciable Taxable Canadian Property

Note: The information you provide on this form is collected under the authority of the *Income Tax Act* (ITA) and is protected by the provisions of the *Privacy Act*. It is used to process requests for certificates of compliance under section 116 of the ITA and is retained in information bank number CRA-OPPU 111.

Vendor (non-resident)

| ☐ Corporation | ☐ Trust | ☐ Partnership | ☐ Individual |

| Business number | Trust account number | Social insurance, individual tax, or subsidiary ledger number |

| Last name (print) | First name and initial (print) | Date of birth YYYY MM DD | Date of departure from Canada (if applicable) YYYY MM DD |

| Present address | | Telephone number |

| Country of residence (see the instructions on page 1) | Fax number |

| Representative name | Telephone number |

| Representative address | Fax number |

Check the box where correspondence is to be sent (if no box is ticked, correspondence will be sent to vendor)   ☐ Vendor   ☐ Representative

Purchaser

| Last name (print) | First name and initial (print) | Telephone number |

| Present address | Fax number |

| Representative name | Telephone number |

| Representative address | Fax number |

Check the box where correspondence is to be sent (if no box is ticked, correspondence will be sent to purchaser)   ☐ Purchaser   ☐ Representative

Details of property (see the instructions on page 1 for more information)

| ☐ Depreciable property | ☐ Real property (other than capital property) | ☐ Canadian resource property | ☐ Timber resource property |

| Date of proposed or completed disposition ▶ YYYY MM DD | Vendor's acquisition date ▶ YYYY MM DD |

| Property jurisdiction ▶ | City/Municipality | Province/territory | Postal code |

Property Description

Gross proceeds of disposition. Tick the box that applies to you   ☐ Proposed disposition   ☐ Completed disposition

(1) Proceeds of Disposition	(2) Capital Cost	(3) Lesser of Column (1) and column (2)	(4) Undepreciated Capital Cost or Cost Amount	(5) Income or (loss) Column (3) minus column (4)	(6) Exemptions	(7) Net Income or (loss) Column (5) minus column (6)
$	$	$	$	$	$	$

Payment of tax. Enter Part 1 federal tax on net income.
(For resource property, enter the amount from line (H) of Form T2062A, Schedule1.)   ▶ $

T2062A E (11/2016)   (Vous pouvez obtenir ce formulaire en français à arc.gc.ca/formulaires.)   Canada

Get The Best Capital Gains Tax Advice

1. Is the disposition subject to an election under section 85 (transfer of property to a company)?		☐ Yes	☐ No

2. Did you rent or lease the property during the period of ownership? ☐ Yes ☐ No
If *yes*, please complete the following:

☐ Non-resident tax was withheld. Provide name and address of person who withheld the tax. ▶

☐ Non-resident tax was not withheld. State the period during which income was received from the property (attach statements that show the amount of gross income).

From: YYYY MM DD   To: YYYY MM DD

If no, state the use of the property during the period of ownership. ▶

3. If you have outstanding balances for taxes, including income or excise taxes, custom duties, or the goods and services tax/harmonized sales tax (GST/HST), provide the identification or account number(s) for the outstanding balances. ▶

4. Indicate the last tax year for which you filed a Canadian income tax return, if applicable. ▶

5. Is the disposition of property to a person with whom you are not dealing with at arm's length, or a gift inter-vivos? ☐ Yes ☐ No
If *yes*, to either or both, and the disposition is at less than fair market value, enter the vendor's share of the fair market value at the time of the disposition in the vendor's share of gross proceeds of disposition column (1) above.

Certification

Please check the box(es) that apply if you are authorizing the CRA to deal with your representative concerning:

☐ T2062A, *Request by a Non-Resident of Canada for a Certificate of Compliance Related to the Disposition of Canadian Resource or Timber Resource Property, Canadian Real Property (Other than Capital Property), or Depreciable Taxable Canadian Property*

☐ T1261, *Application for a CRA Individual Tax Number (ITN) for Non-Residents*

I, _____ , certify that the information given on this form is, to the best of my knowledge, correct and complete.
　　　　Name

_____　　_____　　_____
Date　　　　　　　　(Authorized person's signature)　　　　(Position or office)

27